W9-BYZ-217

Animal TECH

CREEPY & CRAWLY

Tessa Miller

full tilt
PRESS

Creepy & Crawly
Animal Tech

Copyright © 2019

Published by Full Tilt Press
Written by Tessa Miller
All rights reserved.

Printed in the United States of America.

Full Tilt Press
42982 Osgood Road
Fremont, CA 94539
readfulltilt.com
Full Tilt Press publications may be purchased for educational, business, or sales promotional use.

Editorial Credits
Design and layout by Sara Radka
Edited by Renae Gilles
Copyedited by Kristin J. Russo

Image Credits
Getty Images: cover, 3 (robot), 7, 19, 20, 22 (detail), 22, 23 (detail), 25, 31, 35 (detail), 36, 39, 40, background, Dorling Kindersley RF, 16, 16 (detail), EyeEm, 41 (detail), Foam, 38, iStockphoto, 1, 3 (spider), 4, 6, 10, 10 (detail), 12, 17 (background), 18, 28, 29 (detail), 37, 40 (detail), 41, 44, 45, RooM RF, 42, Stocktrek Images, 27; Newscom: Albert Lleal/ Minden Pictures, 28 (detail), dpa/picture-alliance, 3 (gecko foot), dpa/picture-alliance, 26, KRT, 43, Kyodo, 21, 33, MediaforMedical/Jean-Paul Chassenet, 9, NHPA/Photoshot, 30, 32, 34 (detail), wenn.com, 29, zumapress.com, 35; Pixabay: cover; Shutterstock: cover, 3 (termite), 5, 11, 14, 23, 24, 34; Wikimedia: 11 (detail), 17, David Brazier, 13, Dr. Neil Campbell, 8, Gary Bembridge, 15

ISBN: 978-1-62920-738-4 (library binding)
ISBN: 978-1-62920-778-0 (eBook)

CONTENTS

Ants work in groups to build paths, gather food, and protect their homes.

INTRODUCTION

The earth is crawling with creepy and slimy creatures. Scientists think there are more than 8 million different **species** of animals. Eighty percent of those are insects. This means the earth is covered with bugs. They come in all shapes and sizes. Worms can also be found everywhere. They crawl on or under the ground. They sometimes live inside other animals, including humans. There are also about 9,500 species of reptiles. These include snakes, lizards, turtles, alligators, and crocodiles.

That's a lot of creepy and crawly creatures. They have attracted the attention of many scientists. By studying worms, insects, and reptiles, scientists can come up with new **technology**. Scientists made a robot that moves just like a snake. They built a shopping mall modeled after a termite mound. Scientists and **engineers** are copying nature to improve lives. This is called biomimicry. "Bio" means life. "Mimicry" is when you copy something else. Many different technologies have been inspired by the creepiest and crawliest critters on earth.

---

species: a group of plants or animals with similar features

technology: tools and knowledge used to meet a need or solve a problem

engineer: a person who plans and builds tools, machines, or structures

SPINY-HEADED WORM

SKIN GRAFTS

A young spiny-headed worm lives inside an insect. When the insect is eaten by a fish, the worm then moves to live inside the fish.

Injuries, rather than illnesses, are the number-one reason kids visit the emergency room.

Parasitic worms might not seem very helpful. For most people, just thinking about them makes their skin crawl. However, doctors have been inspired by these worms. The worms are helping to make medicine better.

Sometimes doctors see patients with very deep wounds. These wounds need to be sewn back together. Often, doctors sew wounds closed with stitches, or sutures. Sutures use a special type of sewing needle and thread. Sometimes the thread isn't strong enough. Doctors then have to staple wounds closed. But a stapled wound can open up again.

Doctors needed to figure out a better way to treat wounds where sutures and staples didn't work. So they looked to nature and found the spiny-headed worm. This worm latches onto its **host**. It can then stay strongly attached. By mimicking the worm's abilities, doctors are developing a new type of medical patch. The patch would latch on just like a spiny-headed worm. It could hold wounds together more securely. It could also help keep wounds cleaner. This would speed up recovery time.

parasitic: living inside of and getting food from another animal or plant

host: the animal or plant in which a parasite lives

LESSONS FROM NATURE

The spiny-headed worm uses fish as a host. It lives in the fish's intestines. This worm has a special head. It is shaped like a needle. First the worm sticks its head into the intestine. The head then swells up. This keeps the worm stuck in place.

Doctors copied this. They are making a patch that is covered with hundreds of tiny hooks. Each hook acts like a worm's spiny head. The patch is gently pressed into the skin around the wound. The hooks then swell up. This holds the wound closed.

Parasitic worms can be found in almost all animals with a backbone. This includes fish, amphibians, reptiles, birds, and mammals.

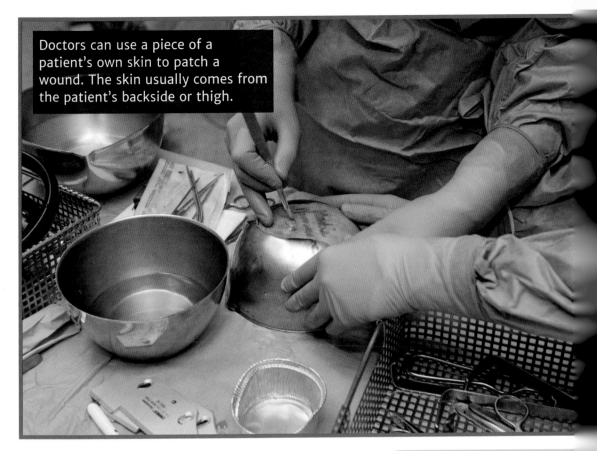

Doctors can use a piece of a patient's own skin to patch a wound. The skin usually comes from the patient's backside or thigh.

Doctors have not tried the patch on patients yet. But they hope the tiny hooks are too small to hurt. They want to use the patch on burn patients. These patients often require skin **grafts**. The patch would hold the grafts more securely.

Doctors also hope to use the patch on wounds inside the body. The patch would work better than sutures. It would stick to these surfaces, just like a parasitic worm.

graft: a piece of skin, muscle, or bone that is moved from one part of the body to another to help it heal

TECH IN ACTION

Parasitic worms can make people sick. But doctors are using them as inspiration for improving medicine.

HEAD
The spiny-headed worm has a head shaped like a needle.

SWELLING
The head swells up after poking a hole in the intestines of a fish.

IN PLACE
The swelling keeps the worm in place until it decides to move.

NEEDLES
The new medical patch has hundreds of tiny needles.

STICKING
The needles swell up when they get wet.

SECURE
The patch stays in place even on wet surfaces.

TERMITE MOUNDS

BUILDINGS

Termites use soil and their own saliva and droppings to build their mounds.

Zimbabwe's Eastgate Centre doesn't have air conditioners. It stays cool thanks to biomimicry.

Have you ever walked upstairs and found that the temperature is hotter than downstairs? That is because hot air rises. When air heats up, it becomes less **dense**. The hot air then floats on top of the cold air. This can be a problem in tall buildings. The hot air rises to the top floors. In very hot places, cooling down the top floors can be tough.

Today, air conditioners are usually used to cool down tall buildings. Sometimes air conditioners run all day and night. This uses a lot of electricity and can be very expensive. Mick Pearce, an architect in Zimbabwe, wanted to solve this problem. Architects are people who **design** buildings.

Mick Pearce looked to nature for a solution. He found termite mounds. These mounds stay cool inside during the hottest part of the day. They also stay warm during the coldest part of the night.

dense: made up of pieces that are packed tightly together

design: to make a plan by thinking about the purpose or use of something

A termite mound is very complex. It includes many tunnels and rooms for food storage.

LESSONS FROM NATURE

Termites keep their mounds cool with a unique **system**. In the middle of the mound, there is a chimney. Hundreds of tiny tunnels are attached to it. The tunnels lead to the outside. During the day, the tunnels fill with hot air. This hot air pushes the cool air down. The cool air goes into the living area of the mound. During the day, the air in the living area slowly warms up. At night, cooler air enters the tunnels. The warmer air in the living area rises. It pushes the cool air back down. This air **current** keeps the living area at a livable temperature.

system: a set of parts that work together

current: a flow of air or water in one direction

Pearce designed Zimbabwe's largest shopping mall, the Eastgate Centre. He copied the termite's system. The roof has vents that act like chimneys. The walls have tubes. They run to the outside of the building. This system creates air currents like a termite mound. It keeps the building cool. It doesn't need to run air conditioners all the time. This saves a lot of money.

DID YOU KNOW?
In one day, temperatures in Zimbabwe can swing from 35° Fahrenheit to 104°F (2° Celsius to 40°C). That's a difference of 70°F (38°C).

The Eastgate Centre is home to many shops and business offices. It covers half a city block.

TECH IN ACTION

How do you keep a large building cool without using a lot of energy? Biomimicry of a termite mound is one way.

CHIMNEY
Termite mounds have a central chimney.

TUNNELS
The tunnels attached to this chimney fill with hot or cold air.

AIR MOVEMENT
Because hot air rises and cold air sinks, the air inside the termite mound is constantly moving.

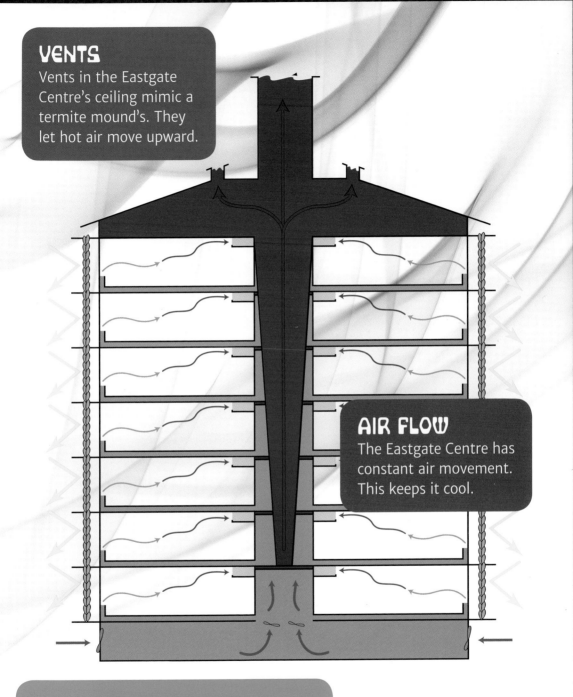

VENTS
Vents in the Eastgate Centre's ceiling mimic a termite mound's. They let hot air move upward.

AIR FLOW
The Eastgate Centre has constant air movement. This keeps it cool.

TUBES
There are hundreds of tubes in the walls of the mall. They let hot and cold air move.

SPIDER WEBS

BULLETPROOF VESTS

A spider makes silk for spinning webs, catching bugs, and laying eggs. The silk is made of proteins. Proteins are basic building blocks of life.

Bulletproof vests are usually made of Kevlar. Kevlar is a type of very strong plastic.

In recent years, there have been wars in some very hot places. Many soldiers fought in the Iraq War (2003–2011). They were faced with temperature highs of 110°F (43°C) in the city of Baghdad.

Soldiers who work in such heat want their clothing to be as light as possible. But instead, they have to wear very thick and heavy uniforms. The uniforms must cover all parts of their body. Soldiers have to wear heavy body armor as well. Body armor protects against bullets. It keeps soldiers safe. It can also make working in hot places very difficult.

Fortunately, there are scientists working for the US military. They are looking at ways to reduce the weight of a soldier's body armor. They are working with one of the strongest **fibers** in the natural world—spider silk.

fiber: a thin thread that is usually used to make something, like fabric

LESSONS FROM NATURE

Spiders make their webs from spider silk. The silk is very stretchy. It can be pulled farther before breaking than any other natural fiber. The silk is also very strong when woven. These thin fibers are also extremely lightweight.

Scientists in the Netherlands have a **lab** crawling with spiders. They created a **material** that mimics spider silk. It looks like human skin. It can stop bullets. In a lab in Michigan, researchers use spiders and silkworms to make very strong silk. Using that silk, they invented a new fabric called Dragon Silk. This fabric could be used to make better bulletproof vests. Dragon Silk is stronger than the vests police officers and soldiers wear today. Making it is also better for the **environment**. No chemicals are needed and no pollution is created.

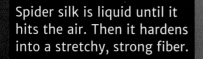

Spider silk is liquid until it hits the air. Then it hardens into a stretchy, strong fiber.

Many research groups and companies around the world are competing to make products from spider silk.

A company in Japan is using microorganisms, tiny living things, to grow silk like a spider's. Now the company can make silk very quickly. They are able to use it to make car parts that are strong but flexible. These parts can help people from getting hurt in accidents.

DID YOU KNOW?
Silkworms build cocoons out of a single strand of silk. These strands can be 3,000 feet (900 meters) long.

lab: a place for doing scientific work (short for laboratory)

material: cloth or fabric, usually before it is made into something

environment: the air, water, plants, animals, weather, and other things in an area

TECH IN ACTION

Spider silk is a unique natural fiber. Scientists are coming up with new ways to use it to help humans.

STRONG
Spider silk is stronger than steel when woven together.

LIGHTWEIGHT
Spider silk is also lightweight.

NATURAL
A spider makes its silk using only natural materials.

TOUGH
Dragon Silk is so strong it can stop bullets.

ECO-FRIENDLY
Making Dragon Silk is better for the environment than other materials, such as Kevlar.

THIN
The material is thin and lightweight. It is easy to layer with other clothing.

GECKOS

ADHESIVE

Geckos are a type of lizard.
There are almost 1,000
different species of gecko.

New high-tech fabrics and materials are called "smart clothes" or "wearable technology."

Geckos are some of the best climbers in the world. These tiny lizards can climb almost anything. They can crawl across trees and ceilings. They can creep along flat and slippery surfaces. What would it be like if a human could climb like this? What if a person could climb a wall using only their hands and feet?

A US military research group wanted to answer these questions. So they started a research **program**. They hired **biologists** to study geckos. From their studies, they have made a new material. They call it Geckskin. This material could be worn by soldiers during missions. It would allow a soldier to climb just like a gecko. They wouldn't need complicated, heavy climbing gear. They wouldn't have to pack rope and a harness. Soldiers could just slip on the Geckskin and climb.

program: a plan or project set up to achieve a long-term goal

biologist: someone who studies living things, such as plants and animals

LESSONS FROM NATURE

Geckos' feet are covered in millions of **microscopic** hairs. These hairs act like little hooks. As the gecko walks, **tendons** that go from the toes to the hairs tense up. The gecko is now latched on. When the gecko wants to move, the tendons relax. The hairs are released, and the gecko moves along.

Geckskin is built to work like this. It has a soft layer of **microfibers**. It mimics a gecko's toes. That layer is covered with a stiff fabric. The fabric acts like the gecko's hairs. It is woven in a special way. This lets it work like the gecko's tendons. A small patch of Geckskin can hold up to 700 pounds (320 kilograms).

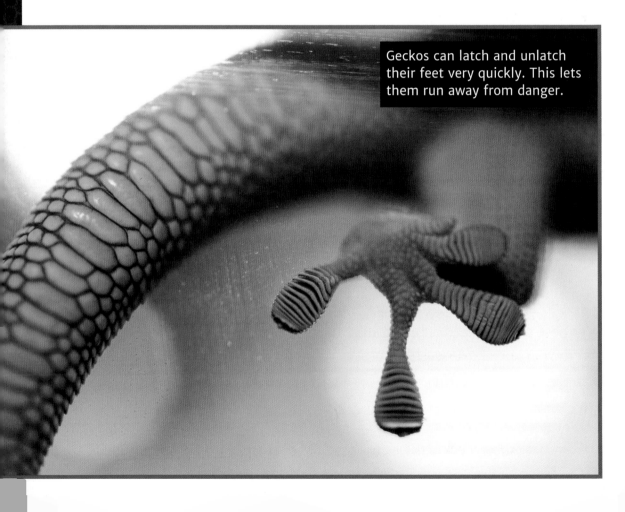

Geckos can latch and unlatch their feet very quickly. This lets them run away from danger.

The military wants soldiers to use Geckskin to climb buildings in cities. They wouldn't have to carry ropes and ladders. With Geckskin, they could move much more quickly and safely.

Scientists plan to use Geckskin for more than climbing up walls. They want to make robots that climb around like a gecko. But these robots would climb around in space, on the outside of a spaceship.

microscopic: very tiny; only able to be seen with a microscope

tendon: a stringy piece of tissue connecting muscles, bones, and other parts of the body

microfiber: a very fine fiber that is not natural but is made by humans

TECH IN ACTION

A gecko can crawl and climb using only its feet. By wearing Geckskin, people can do the same thing.

TRACTION

Geckos can climb vertical surfaces, like walls. They can even climb on ceilings.

TINY HAIRS

Geckos have thousands of tiny hairs on their feet. These act like hooks.

TENDONS

Each hair has a tendon. It forces the hair to cling to a surface.

GRIP
With Geckskin, a person can climb straight up or hang upside down.

MICROFIBERS
Thousands of microfibers help Geckskin cling to a surface.

FABRIC
A layer of stiff fabric holds each microfiber in place.

SNAKES

ROBOTS

There are more than 3,000 different species of snake. Since none of them have legs or feet, they all use their muscles and scales to move.

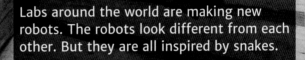

Labs around the world are making new robots. The robots look different from each other. But they are all inspired by snakes.

A building has collapsed after a powerful earthquake. Rescuers have been sent in to search for people. Survivors are crying out for help. But the rescuers can't reach them. The way is blocked by **debris**.

Luckily, scientists at a lab in Pennsylvania have designed a robot that can help. It is shaped like a snake. This robot can slither into small places. It can also climb. It can move faster than even the fastest snake.

Using the robot, searchers can stay safe while the robot winds its way through danger. It can be **programmed** to explore areas on its own. People can also control it with a remote.

The researchers who invented these robots don't call their work biomimicry. They are inspired by nature, but they aren't copying it. They are taking something in nature and making it even better. They call this "bioinspiration."

---

debris: remains left after destruction

program: to give a piece of technology a set of instructions to do a certain task

LESSONS FROM NATURE

The lab calls its robots **modular** snake robots. They tested the first modular snake robot in many different places, from rain forests to frozen lakes. It could successfully move over almost any type of land. But it did not work in deep sand. It could not gain traction when the sand moved under its weight. So scientists had to find an animal that could walk on top of sand.

Researchers looked to sidewinder snakes in Arizona for help. These snakes have a unique way of slithering. They squish their bodies as flat as they can. Then they twist in a zigzag pattern. The motion lets the snakes travel across the sand, even when the sand is moving. It also lets them easily climb sand dunes.

This was a **breakthrough** for the scientists. They created a modular snake robot that mimics the sidewinder's twist. This robot can now go anywhere. It can be used for search and rescue. The robot could save many lives during a disaster.

Sidewinders are a type of rattlesnake. They bite and are venomous.

Researchers in Japan built a robot that can climb through pipes. It can be used to reach people after earthquakes.

modular: made up of many pieces that can come together in different ways

breakthrough: a sudden discovery that leads to an increase in knowledge

DID YOU KNOW?

A snake robot is built in sections. Each section carries special items. People can add sections to the robot if it needs to do more than one thing on a mission.

TECH IN ACTION

To build a search-and-rescue robot, engineers mimicked the body and movement of a snake.

FORM
Snakes are skinny and very flexible.

MANEUVERABILITY
Snakes move forward and backward, swim, and climb without feet or hands.

SURFACES
Sidewinder snakes can zigzag up steep sand dunes.

SHAPE
Scientists made the modular robot in the shape of a snake.

AREAS
Scientists can program the robots to swim, climb, and zigzag through any area.

MOBILITY
While some use tracks, snake-like robots move without wheels or wings.

ANTS

ANTIVIRUS SOFTWARE

Ants are excellent problem solvers. Engineers, architects, math experts, and computer scientists study them to solve human problems.

Computer viruses are malicious. This means they are made to do harm, such as steal information.

Ants aren't very big. The common black ant is only about 0.2 inches (0.5 centimeters) long. Ants have to work together to survive. They live together in **colonies** or nests. There are hundreds, even thousands, of ants per colony. Each ant has a job. By working together and doing their jobs, ants can be very powerful. Sometimes other animals attack an ant colony. The colony fights back.

Computers work like an ant colony. There are thousands of pieces in a computer. This includes hardware, such as the screen and keyboard. It also includes **software**. Each piece has its own job. When the pieces are working together, computers can get a lot done.

But when something attacks a computer, such as a virus, it cannot fight back. Computer attacks are becoming a big problem around the world. Researchers are working to change this. They are making software that would fight back. The software mimics how ants protect their colony.

---

colony: a group of people or animals that live together

software: computer programs

LESSONS FROM NATURE

People already use software to protect their computers. The software **scans** for viruses. But if it scans all the time, it slows down the computer. It can also scan once a night or once a week. But this leaves the computer open to attack during the time the program is not scanning. So researchers from North Carolina and Washington state made a new antivirus software. It uses digital "ants" to protect the computer.

In an ant colony, there are scouts. They go off in search of food. If they find something, they go back to the colony and signal to the other ants. Then a large group goes to collect the food. Ant colonies also have soldier ants. They attack things that might hurt the colony. Like the ant colony, the antivirus software first sends out scouts. These digital scouts wander the computer system. If they find a virus, they send signals to other digital ants. Those ants then attack the virus.

After an attack on an ant colony, builder ants come to fix any damage. The new software does this too.

Soldier ants attack to protect their colony. They might also attack to get food.

Large companies often hire computer scientists. They work to protect computer systems from viruses and other attacks.

This new software scans constantly. But it only uses a few digital ants at a time. It doesn't slow a computer down. This means it can send lots of ants in quickly to attack when they are needed.

DID YOU KNOW?

One of the largest known ant colonies is in Europe. It stretches for 3,700 miles (6,000 kilometers) underground.

scan: to look at or study carefully in order to find something

TECH IN ACTION

Ants are small, but they are powerful when in a large group. A new antivirus software mimics how ants protect their colony.

PATROL
Scout ants constantly patrol the colony.

SWARM
When there is a problem, soldier ants swarm together to help fix it.

REPAIR
Builder ants then repair any damage done to the colony.

MONITORING
Antivirus software "ants" monitor the computer's systems.

ATTACK
If a virus is detected, the software sends many more "ants" to attack it.

FIX
After the attack, the software repairs the computer.

CREEPY & CRAWLY

CONCLUSION

A snake flicks its tongue to taste chemicals in the air. It uses the information to build a map of its environment.

Scientists continue to build snake robots. New robots can respond to chemicals in the environment.

Even the creepiest animals can improve technology. The study of worms, insects, and reptiles has made people's lives better. It has led to many new inventions. This includes medical patches that latch wounds together. These patches could help people heal faster after injury. Geckskin could allow humans to scale walls like a gecko. Bulletproof vests of the future could be made of spider silk. These technologies wouldn't be possible if scientists hadn't used biomimicry.

New technologies are exciting and can do a lot of good. But they are also **risky**. Snake-like robots could be used by criminals. They could be used for spying or stealing. Geckskin suits could also be used for spying. Or they could be used to help break into buildings. Scientists continue to change the world by studying creepy and crawly creatures. Who knows what new inventions might creep up next?

risky: having a chance of something bad happening

ACTIVITY

EXPLORE ANIMAL FEET

How do mountain goats cling to rocks? How do penguins keep from slipping on ice? Try this activity to explore how animals' feet help them gain traction on different surfaces. You can test different shoes to figure out how they grip.

WHAT YOU NEED

- Shoes with different types of soles. These can be cleats, ballet slippers, tennis shoes, high heels, hiking boots, snow boots, flip flops, etc.

- Different surfaces to walk on. This can include carpet, a gym floor, linoleum, wood, pavement, gravel, grass, mud, etc.

- a pencil and paper

WHAT TO DO

1. Break up into equal teams. In your group, examine at least three pairs of shoes. Write down what surface you think they would be best for walking on.

2. Brainstorm animals from different environments. Think about what type of feet they have. Compare them to the shoes you examined. How are they similar? How are they different?

3. Next, conduct a walking experiment. Have a group member walk on each surface. Use each pair of shoes. Keep track of which shoes worked best on each surface, being careful not to slip and fall.

4. After all teams have tried this, compare notes.

5. Which shoes worked best on which surfaces? Was there a shoe that didn't help you walk on any surface? Return to your list of animals. Which animal would walk best on these surfaces? Do their feet match the soles of the shoes?

GLOSSARY

biologist: someone who studies living things, such as plants and animals

breakthrough: a sudden discovery that leads to an increase in knowledge

colony: a group of people or animals that live together

current: a flow of air or water in one direction

debris: remains left after destruction

dense: made up of pieces that are packed tightly together

design: to make a plan by thinking about the purpose or use of something

engineer: a person who plans and builds tools, machines, or structures

environment: the air, water, plants, animals, weather, and other things in an area

fiber: a thin thread that is usually used to make something, like fabric

graft: a piece of skin, muscle, or bone that is moved from one part of the body to another to help it heal

host: the animal or plant in which a parasite lives

lab: a place for doing scientific work (short for laboratory)

material: cloth or fabric, usually before it is made into something

microfiber: a very fine fiber that is not natural but is made by humans

microscopic: very tiny; only able to be seen with a microscope

modular: made up of many pieces that can come together in different ways

parasitic: living inside of and getting food from another animal or plant

program (pg 25): a plan or project set up to achieve a long-term goal

program (pg 31): to give a piece of technology a set of instructions to do a certain task

risky: having a chance of something bad happening

scan: to look at or study carefully in order to find something

software: computer programs

species: a group of plants or animals with similar features

system: a set of parts that work together

technology: tools and knowledge used to meet a need or solve a problem

tendon: a stringy piece of tissue connecting muscles, bones, and other parts of the body

READ MORE

Becker, Helaine. *Zoobots: Wild Robots Inspired by Real Animals.* Toronto: Kids Can Press, 2014.

Holzweiss, Kristina. *Amazing Makerspace DIY Basic Machines.* New York: Children's Press, 2017.

Jenkins, Steve and Robin Page. *Creature Features: 25 Animals Explain Why They Look the Way They Do.* Boston: Houghton Mifflin Harcourt, 2014.

Yomtov, Nelson. *From Termite Den to . . . Office Building.* Innovations from Nature. Ann Arbor, Mich.: Cherry Lake Publishing, 2014.

Yamada, Kobi. *What Do You Do with an Idea?* Seattle: Compendium Kids, 2013.

WEBSITES

https://ww2.kqed.org/quest/2008/10/21/bio-inspiration-nature-as-muse/

Visit a biomimicry lab.

https://www.sciencenewsforstudents.org/article/flu-fighter-found-frog-slime

Learn how frog slime can treat the flu.

http://www.pbs.org/wgbh/nova/next/tech/evolution-of-bioinspired-robots/

Read about the history of biomimicry robots.

http://thekidshouldseethis.com/post/sciencetake-the-secrets-of-a-sidewinder-snake-on-a-sandy-slope

Watch a video of sidewinder snake movement.

https://kids.nwf.org/Home/Kids/Ranger-Rick/Animals/Insects-and-Arthropods/Ants-Rule.aspx

Learn about the secret lives of ants.

https://www.amnh.org/explore/science-topics/nature-as-innovator/bioinspiration-quiz

Play a game matching animals to technologies.

INDEX